Patterdale Terrier Tricks Training

Patterdale Terrier Tricks & Games Training Tracker & Workbook.
Includes: Patterdale Terrier Multi-Level Tricks, Games & Agility.

Part 3

Training Central

Copyright © 2023

All rights reserved. Without limiting rights under the copyright reserved above, no part of this publication may be reproduced, stored, introduced into a retrieval system, distributed or transmitted in any form or by any means, including without limitation photocopying, recording, or other electronic or mechanical methods, without the prior written permission of the publisher, except in the case of brief quotations embodied in critical reviews and certain other non-commercial uses permitted by copyright law.

The scanning, uploading, and/or distribution of this document via the internet or via any other means without the permission of the publisher is illegal and is punishable by law. Please purchase only authorized editions and do not participate in or encourage electronic piracy of copyrightable materials.

Introductory Note

Welcome to this interactive tricks workbook.

We want to start by thanking all of the Patterdale Terrier fans out there whom inspired us to complete this three part series in which we cover a variety of tricks and games that you can teach your Patterdale Terrier.

Our intention is for you to learn and grow with your beloved Patterdale Terrier whilst having a great time. We trust that you will enjoy and benefit from the use of the books in this series.

Be sure to make notes on the pages found after each trick. We found this supports learning significantly.

Have fun whilst you log and note down your progress, any new ideas, thoughts, techniques that work for you/new methods, or even sketches.

Good luck and wishing you all the best.

Table of Contents

Go To the Crate 4

Carry an Object 7

Tidy Up Your Toys 10

Roll In a Blanket 13

Are You Scared? 16

Who's a Brave Dog? 19

Kiss Me 22

Speak 25

Shaping the Retrieve 28

Helpful Notes: Links and Chains 31

Go Get Your Leash 34

Get the Mail/Newspaper 37

Go Find the Remote 40

Go Get the Phone 43

Go Get Your Dish 46

Find My Car Keys Please 49

Put Away Your Toys 52

Bring This to Daddy 55

Mail a Letter 58

Throw This in the Trash 61

Let's Play Ring Toss 64

Sea Hunt 67

Achoo! Can I Have a Tissue? 70

Show Me Your Best Side 73

Push a Baby Carriage 76

Hi-Ho Silver, Away! 79

Sit Up Pretty 82

Balance a Cookie on Your Nose 85

Say You're Sorry 88

Say Your Prayers 91

Ring a Bell 94

Dancing Patterdale Terrier 97

Get Me a Bottle of Water - Part 1 100

Get Me a Bottle of Water - Part 2 103

Get Me a Bottle of Water - Part 3 106

Go Left, Go Right 109

Find It 112

Weave Poles 115

Jump Hurdle 118

Through Hoop/Tunnel 121

Weave Through Legs 124

Jump Through Arms 127

Go To the Crate

1. Hold the crate door open and verbally encourage your Patterdale Terrier to go inside. He may act curious and sniff around it while you hold the door open.

2. If he manages to go inside, praise him, pet him and give him treats to show that this is positive behavior.

3. Don't close the crate door unless he is comfortable inside. Shutting him in will only make this command feel like a punishment.

4. Introduce him to the command "Go to crate" throughout the exercise, continue saying it whenever he does go inside.

5. Lure him by placing his favorite treats and toys inside the crate to get his attention. As you make progress, place the treats further inside the crate so that he has to go inside to get them.

6. Practice the "Go to crate" command until he learns the behavior that you expect of him.

How did you get on? What challenges did you face & how did you overcome them? What could you do better for next time? **Any new discoveries?** Funny moments? *Memorable Photos?* **Sketches?**
Any other thoughts, comments or feedback

Carry an Object

1. Command your Patterdale Terrier to stand or sit in front of you when you begin training. Only attempt this trick if your Patterdale Terrier is used to holding objects in his mouth without chewing them up.

2. Start training with objects that you won't mind being chewed up such as a newspaper.

3. Hold the object towards his nose and when he begins sniffing it, click.

4. Click again when your Patterdale Terrier begins displaying an interest in the object such as by licking it or butting it.

5. When he opens his mouth toward the object, click again to show him that he is doing the right thing.

6. Once your Patterdale Terrier opens his mouth over the object, gradually pull it away then click only when he follows then grabs it.

7. When he finally grabs it and holds the object in his mouth, click and praise him as you hold the object on the other end.

8. Practice this command until you get your Patterdale Terrier to hold the object for up to 4 seconds.

How did you get on? What challenges did you face & how did you overcome them? What could you do better for next time? **Any new discoveries?** Funny moments? *Memorable Photos?* **Sketches?**

Any other thoughts, comments or feedback

Tidy Up Your Toys

1. Compile all of your Patterdale Terrier's toys in a basket or a box.

2. Point to a toy as you give the "take it" command followed by "bring it" and "drop it" as you guide him to the basket. Each time he successfully drops a toy into the basket, click, then reward him.

3. Once all toys are placed away, give him more treats and use the verbal command "Put your toys away".

4. Continue practicing this several times until your Patterdale Terrier understands "Put your toys away"; ensure that you give him a significant reward such as his favorite treat each time.

5. Help him master this trick more efficiently by putting toys farther away each time; as you work with him in locating the toys and placing them in the basket with your command.

How did you get on? What challenges did you face & how did you overcome them? What could you do better for next time? **Any new discoveries?** Funny moments? *Memorable Photos?* **Sketches?**
Any other thoughts, comments or feedback

Roll In a Blanket

1. Begin the training with your Patterdale Terrier lying down, then place a spacious blanket next to him.

2. Offer him a corner of the blanket and say the "take it" command. Click and treat when he takes the corner into his mouth.

3. When your Patterdale Terrier masters steps 1 and 2, instruct him to "roll over" when the blanket is in his mouth. Click and treat each time he successfully follows the "roll over" command.

4. Continue practicing this until he learns to do steps 1-3 in one smooth motion.

5. Transition from using "roll over" to "nap time" and work on it until your Patterdale Terrier learns to roll himself in the blanket with the "nap time" cue.

How did you get on? What challenges did you face & how did you overcome them? What could you do better for next time? **Any new discoveries?** Funny moments? *Memorable Photos?* **Sketches?**

Any other thoughts, comments or feedback

Are You Scared?

1. This trick will put a smile on everyone's faces, especially children. To indicate his "fright," your pup will run under a table or bed and peek out from under the tablecloth or bedspread. The steps for teaching this trick are as follows:

1. Start with your Patterdale Terrier under the table, and use your voice or a treat to get him to peek out. Click and treat.

2. Make sure you time your click for when he first pushes out from under the cloth.

3. Repeat this six to eight times and then try putting him under again and wait to see if he offers peeking out on his own.

4. Once your Patterdale Terrier has this part down, teach him to go under the table using a target lid.

5. Bait the target with a treat at first to encourage him to go under the tablecloth and click and treat each time.

6. Take the bait off the target but leave the target under the table or bed and send him back again. Click and treat your Patterdale Terrier for going under the table or bed after the target.

7. To get the peeking behavior, repeat the above step (getting him under the object) until he offers it readily and then delay the click. When your Patterdale Terrier doesn't hear the click, he will probably come back out to see what's wrong. Click and treat him just as he peeks out from under the cloth.. Repeat this until he runs under and peeks out readily; then verbally label the behavior "Are You Scared?"

Note: What if My Patterdale Terrier Doesn't Peek?

If you are having trouble getting your Patterdale Terrier to peek because he runs all the way out from under the tablecloth or bedspread, it means that you need to click sooner: An early click will catch him just as he is emerging and give him the idea that peeking is what is being clicked.

How did you get on? What challenges did you face & how did you overcome them? What could you do better for next time? **Any new discoveries?** Funny moments? *Memorable Photos?* **Sketches?**
Any other thoughts, comments or feedback

Who's a Brave Dog?

This trick is similar to "Are You Scared?" except in this trick your Patterdale Terrier will run around behind the handler and through his legs until he is looking up at the handler's face. The shaping steps to teach "Who's a Brave Dog?" are as follows:

1. Starting with your Patterdale Terrier sitting in front of you, use a target stick to get your Patterdale Terrier to go around you to the left or right.

2. Practice this until your Patterdale Terrier will run behind your legs and touch the target for a click and treat.

3. Slowly move the target between your feet so that he goes between your legs enough to be able to look up at you.

4. Withhold the click after your Patterdale Terrier starts to catch on to going through your legs and see if he will look up at you, then click and treat.

5. If your Patterdale Terrier runs all the way through your legs, use the target stick to show him where to stop and click and treat him before he actually touches it.

6. You can label this behavior as "Who's a Brave Dog?" by saying it right before you give the cue that starts the behavior, like pointing or whatever you did to encourage him to go around you.

7. Slowly fade the target as your Patterdale Terrier starts to offer the behavior readily by showing the target to get him started and then making the target disappear.

8. Add distractions and be sure to go back to helping your Patterdale Terrier with the target stick if the behavior doesn't remain.

How did you get on? What challenges did you face & how did you overcome them? What could you do better for next time? **Any new discoveries?** Funny moments? *Memorable Photos?* **Sketches?**
Any other thoughts, comments or feedback

Kiss Me

The shaping steps for teaching "Kiss Me" are:

1. Use food initially to excite your Patterdale Terrier. This is key. Feed him a few small pieces of a treat and eat a few yourself, then stick your chin out and wait.

2. At the first sign of any attempt to open his mouth to lick you, click and treat.

3. Try putting the treats in your mouth and showing him they are there. Click and treat any attempt to lick you.

4. Add the verbal cue Kiss right before you think he's going to offer the behavior. Click and treat as the behavior happens.

5. Fade the food by showing it to him and putting it away on a counter or table and commanding Kiss. When he kisses, click and treat and run and get the treat.

6. Repeat this until your Patterdale Terrier is beginning to offer the kiss as soon as you stick out your chin.

How did you get on? What challenges did you face & how did you overcome them? What could you do better for next time? **Any new discoveries?** Funny moments? *Memorable Photos?* **Sketches?**
Any other thoughts, comments or feedback

Speak

Luring and free shaping, or a combination of the two, are the best tools for teaching this trick. The trick itself requires your Patterdale Terrier to bark on cue.

1. Find something that causes your Patterdale Terrier to bark, like a knock on the door or holding a treat out of range. Click and treat him when he barks.

2. Repeat at least twenty to twenty-five times.

3. Fake the initiating action for the barking (the knock or the treat out at range), and if your Patterdale Terrier starts to bark, click and treat.

4. Verbally label the behavior Speak just before your Patterdale Terrier barks.

5. Don't click and treat for any barking other than the one you ask for.

6. If he barks at inappropriate times, be obvious about turning your upper body away to let him know that extraneous barking will not be rewarded.

After basic obedience training skills (Sit, Stay, and Come), these simple tricks are the best opportunity for you and your Patterdale Terrier to build a trusting and cooperative relationship. You will develop a better understanding of how your Patterdale Terrier thinks, and what motivates him, and he will also learn to read your cues. Take the time to train your Patterdale Terrier well; the benefits will last a lifetime!

How did you get on? What challenges did you face & how did you overcome them? What could you do better for next time? **Any new discoveries?** Funny moments? *Memorable Photos?* **Sketches?**
Any other thoughts, comments or feedback

Shaping the Retrieve

To shape the process of retrieving, it best to break it down into small steps. When teaching a Patterdale Terrier to retrieve it is best to pick an easy object to start with - something he is likely to pick up on his own. If you're not sure what texture appeals to your Patterdale Terrier, set out a bunch of objects and see which he chooses to play with on his own - most won't like to pick up metal and have difficulty picking up small objects that require them to smoosh their nose into the floor trying to get their mouth around it. Choose something he can get his mouth around easily, such as a face cloth, a retrieving dumbbell, or a small empty box.

Note 1: Retrieving Dummies

When teaching your Patterdale Terrier to retrieve, start with a novel object that is lightweight but is not a toy or ball. Retrieving dummies are ideal for this purpose. You can find them in pet supply shops.

Teach the retrieve by breaking it down into the most basic steps. The more specific you are with each step, the more likely that the behavior will be retained. The steps to teach the retrieve are as follows:

1. Put an item on the floor about three feet away from your Patterdale Terrier.

2. Click and treat him for moving toward it.

3. Click and treat him for touching the object with his nose.

4. Repeat this step about a dozen times and then withhold the click.

5. If he mouths the object at all, click and treat.

6. Once your Patterdale Terrier is mouthing the object, withhold the click until he picks up the object.

7. Delay the click once more and build the time he will hold the object.

8. Add distance by putting the object a short distance away at first and gradually increasing it.

9. Label the retrieve "Take It" as your Patterdale Terrier is picking up the object.

10. Label the release of the object "Give/Leave It".

Note 2: Retrieval Jackpot

Wait for your Patterdale Terrier to get frustrated enough to close his mouth on the object before you click and treat. More than likely he will mouth the object quickly and release it so be ready to click and give a jackpot.

How did you get on? What challenges did you face & how did you overcome them? What could you do better for next time? **Any new discoveries?** Funny moments? *Memorable Photos?* **Sketches?**
Any other thoughts, comments or feedback

Helpful Notes: Links and Chains

As tricks get more complicated, you begin to understand that one command really represents several behaviors - a behavior chain. In training your Patterdale Terrier to perform these more complicated tasks, you can use two approaches: the behavior chain or back chaining. The main difference is whether you start with first things first or work your way backward from a successful conclusion.

Behavior Chains

The concept of a behavior chain is relatively simple: A behavior chain is simply the breakdown of what needs to be performed in order to complete the behavior. For example, in order for your Patterdale Terrier to bring his leash to you on the command "Go Get Your Leash", he must: know where to find the leash; take it in his mouth (which may mean picking it up off the floor or pulling it from a doorknob); carry it to you in his mouth; and release it into your hand. Each of these steps is a link in the behavior chain, which is only as strong as its weakest element.

Trick Tips: Comfortable Retrieving

Make sure your Patterdale Terrier is comfortable retrieving all of the objects you give him. If the retrieving part of the trick is not taught thoroughly then you will risk your pup not being comfortable at this stage and the performance of the trick will become sloppy and unreliable.

If your Patterdale Terrier requires a lot of additional commands and prompting in order to carry objects, behavior-chain tricks will be choppy and uninteresting. Breaking things down into their component parts is a way of simplifying the trick and improving your pup's performance.

Back Chaining

Back chaining is related to behavior chains except instead of training step 1, step 2, step 3, and so on, you train backwards (step 3, step 2, step 1). The idea is that if you train your Patterdale Terrier backwards and he will perform the behavior more reliably and with greater speed and enthusiasm because he is moving toward something he already knows well. By teaching him a multi-step task backwards, you are helping him to remember the steps more easily because he learned the last one first. So in the case of the trick "Bring Me Your Leash", the sequence would be: "hold the leash and release it into my hand"; "carry the leash to me from a distance"; "take it in your mouth"; "go find it".

Each of these steps may need to be broken down further to meet your pup's individual needs, but the basic concept is the same. When he performs the whole trick, he will be moving from less familiar steps to more familiar steps. Because he learned the last part of the trick first, he will be more confident and flashy as he gets to the end and more reliable overall in his performance of the trick.

Quick Tips: Change Props

If your Patterdale Terrier has difficulty picking up any of the props you are using don't be afraid to go back to the basic steps of the retrieve using the new object. You will find that going back to kindergarten will help his overall grasp of retrieving and will make him more likely to cooperate.

How did you get on? What challenges did you face & how did you overcome them? What could you do better for next time? **Any new discoveries?** Funny moments? *Memorable Photos?* **Sketches?**
Any other thoughts, comments or feedback

Go Get Your Leash

This trick involves having your Patterdale Terrier retrieve his leash and bring it to you. To make this easier on your pup, you may want to have one place where you always leave his leash, such as on a doorknob or by the front door. Your Patterdale Terrier has to go to where the leash is kept and pull the leash off with his mouth. He then needs to carry the leash to you and hold it until you take it from him.

Quick Tips: Should You Throw a Retrieval Object?

The aim of the exercises in this section is to train your Patterdale Terrier to retrieve specific, stationary objects. Throwing objects, as you would in fetch, will put him into prey drive, a highly charged emotional state. It is best to leave the object stationary and let him figure out which behaviors are rewardable and which are not, through your clicking.

If you teach this trick and the following behaviors using back chaining, you will find it easier for your Patterdale Terrier to perform them because he is always moving toward the more familiar steps.

1. Hold the leash out and ask your Patterdale Terrier to take it. Click and treat the exact moment he puts it in his mouth.

2. Back up a step and see if he will follow you; click and treat him for moving with the leash in his mouth.

3. Put the leash on the floor and tell him to "Take It". As soon as he picks it up, click and treat.

4. Put the leash on the floor but don't click and treat until he takes it and takes several steps toward you.

5. Put the leash in various places at various distances and repeat. Click and treat your Patterdale Terrier for taking it under these new circumstances.

6. Gradually move the leash to where your Patterdale Terrier can expect to find it and click and treat him for going to that spot.

7. Replace the "Take It" cue with "Leash", by saying the new cue "Leash" right before the old cue. Gradually fade "Take It" so that your pup will perform the behavior on the new cue.

Special Items

When you are training for retrieving exercises, use an object that you can put away when the session is over; Keep the item "special," so that your Patterdale Terrier looks forward to working with it every time you practice.

How did you get on? What challenges did you face & how did you overcome them? What could you do better for next time? **Any new discoveries?** Funny moments? *Memorable Photos?* **Sketches?**
Any other thoughts, comments or feedback

Get the Mail/Newspaper

This trick works well if you have a door slot for your mail or you have a daily newspaper that gets delivered to your door. For this trick, your Patterdale Terrier has to go to where the mail or paper is kept, pick up the item, bring it to you, and release it into your hand.

1. Teach your Patterdale Terrier to carry non-essential letters and junk mail without stopping to shred them before you use the real thing. ("The dog ate the mortgage bill" probably won't go down well with your spouse.) Do this by clicking and treating your Patterdale Terrier for taking the letter or newspaper and holding it without mouthing it.

2. Take a step or two away and have him bring it to you. Click and treat the motion of moving toward you.

3. Put the letter on the floor and tell your Patterdale Terrier to "Take It". You may want to use junk mail for this part until he refines his techniques in picking up something so close to the floor.

4. When your Patterdale Terrier is retrieving well, begin to work him with the real mail pile or newspaper.

5. Label this behavior "Mail" or "Paper" by saying this new cue right before the current cue "Take It"; pretty soon your Patterdale Terrier will be fetching with enthusiasm and finesse.

How did you get on? What challenges did you face & how did you overcome them? What could you do better for next time? **Any new discoveries?** Funny moments? *Memorable Photos?* **Sketches?**
Any other thoughts, comments or feedback

Go Find the Remote

Visitors - especially those who have only a mild interest in dogs absolutely love this trick. Guests are impressed when a dog can serve a useful purpose. If your housemate tends to hog the remote control, your Patterdale Terrier can be your advocate in getting it back with a smile. For this trick, your Patterdale Terrier has to find the remote, pick it up, carry it to you, and drop it in your hand.

1. Hand your Patterdale Terrier the remote and click and treat him for holding it.

2. Back away a step or two and click and treat him for carrying it to you.

3. Put the remote on the couch or coffee table and tell your Patterdale Terrier to "Take It". Click and treat him for picking it up in his mouth.

4. Send him into the living room at greater distances and click and treat him when he finds the remote.

5. Call him to you as he gets the hang of this and click and treat him for holding it until you reach out to take it.

6. Replace "Take It" with the command "Remote" by offering the new cue right before the old cue.

How did you get on? What challenges did you face & how did you overcome them? What could you do better for next time? **Any new discoveries?** Funny moments? *Memorable Photos?* **Sketches?**
Any other thoughts, comments or feedback

Go Get the Phone

Nothing is better than having your own personal answering service. For this trick your Patterdale Terrier has to retrieve the phone and bring it back to you. You may want to use a cordless phone for this (unless you sit close by) and store it on a low table or the floor to make it easy for him to reach it.

1. Hand your Patterdale Terrier the receiver and tell him to "Take It". Click and treat him for taking it in his mouth and holding it for a few seconds.

2. Hand your Patterdale Terrier the phone and back away from him, encouraging him to follow you. Click and treat him for carrying the phone to you. Make sure the click happens while he is moving towards you, not when he arrives.

3. Repeat this step again, but now click and treat your Patterdale Terrier for delivering the phone to you.

4. Put the phone on the floor and ask him to "Take It"; click and treat him for picking the phone up.

5. Place the phone at greater distances and have him retrieve it from farther away. Time the click and treat for when your Patterdale Terrier puts his mouth on the phone.

6. Increase the difficulty by delaying the click until he has the phone and is turning back to you. You can use a voice prompt like his name or the "Come" command.

7. Label the behavior "Go Get the Phone" by saying it right before the commands "Take It" and "Come", until you can gradually fade the old commands and replace them with the new command "Go Get the Phone".

8. Practice in short sessions until your Patterdale Terrier begins to move towards the phone on the command "Go Get the Phone".

Quick Tip: Use an Old Phone First

Using a cordless phone for this trick is ideal. However if you're afraid that your Patterdale Terrier might chew your good phone to shreds, you might want to start practicing with the receiver from an old phone first. Switch to the real phone once you feel confident that your Patterdale Terrier is good at picking up the receiver without damaging it. Also make sure the real phone is easily accessible to prevent your Patterdale Terrier from dropping it or knocking it off the table.

How did you get on? What challenges did you face & how did you overcome them? What could you do better for next time? **Any new discoveries?** Funny moments? *Memorable Photos?* **Sketches?**

Any other thoughts, comments or feedback

Go Get Your Dish

This trick is a great way to show off your Patterdale Terrier's intelligence. You will probably want to keep his food dish in one spot so that he knows where to go to get it. For this trick your Patterdale Terrier goes and brings his empty dish to you. Your Patterdale Terrier may find it hard to retrieve metal dishes, in which case use a plastic one instead. The shaping steps are as follows:

1. Hand your Patterdale Terrier his dish and tell him to "Take It". Click and treat him for holding the dish.

2. Take a step away and call him to you. Click and treat him for moving toward you with the dish in his mouth.

3. Put the dish on the floor and tell him to "Take It"; click and treat him for picking up the dish.

4. Repeat this step but back away and click and treat him for picking up the dish and moving toward you.

5. Put the dish closer and closer to where you normally keep it, and send him to take it over greater distances.

6. As your Patterdale Terrier improves at this, replace "Take It" with the new verbal cue "Want to Eat?" by saying the new cue right before the old cue, until he starts the behavior on the new cue.

How did you get on? What challenges did you face & how did you overcome them? What could you do better for next time? **Any new discoveries?** Funny moments? *Memorable Photos?* **Sketches?**
Any other thoughts, comments or feedback

Find My Car Keys Please

If you are somebody who constantly loses their keys, this trick may save you a lot of time. For this trick your Patterdale Terrier has to locate your keys by using his eyes and sense of smell, pick them up, bring them to you, and release them to your outstretched hand.

1. Hand your Patterdale Terrier a set of your keys and tell him to "Take It". Click and treat him for holding your keys.

2. Take a few steps back and call him to you. Click and treat him for moving toward you with the keys in his mouth.

3. Put the keys on the floor and tell him to "Take It"; click and treat him for picking up the keys.

4. Repeat the previous step but back away, and click and treat him for picking up the keys and moving toward you.

5. Put the keys in different places at varying distances and click and treat your Patterdale Terrier for finding them. Vary where you put them, sometimes leaving them out in the open, sometimes leaving them concealed.

6. Gradually work it so that your Patterdale Terrier is actively searching for your keys. When you are at this point, label it "Keys". Replace "Take It" by giving the new cue "Keys" right before the old cue. Then, gradually fade the old cue.

7. Practice this one frequently to keep your Patterdale Terrier motivated about searching for your keys.

How did you get on? What challenges did you face & how did you overcome them? What could you do better for next time? **Any new discoveries?** Funny moments? *Memorable Photos?* **Sketches?**
Any other thoughts, comments or feedback

Put Away Your Toys

For this trick your Patterdale Terrier has to pick up one toy at a time and put it in his toy box or basket. The shaping steps are as follows:

1. Hand your Patterdale Terrier a toy and tell him to "Take It"; when he has the toy in his mouth, click and treat him for holding it.

2. Put the toy box between your feet and encourage him to come to you; click and treat him for holding the toy over the top of the box.

3. Repeat the above steps, but ask him to "Leave It" as he holds the toy over the box.

4. Put the toy on the floor and tell him to "Take It"; click and treat him for picking up the toy.

5. Repeat the above step with more than one toy on the floor at a time.

6. Replace the "Take It" and "Leave It" cues with the new cue "Toys Away" by saying the new cue right before the old cue. Gradually fade the old cue.

How did you get on? What challenges did you face & how did you overcome them? What could you do better for next time? **Any new discoveries?** Funny moments? *Memorable Photos?* **Sketches?**
Any other thoughts, comments or feedback

Bring This to Daddy

This trick is great for your Patterdale Terrier if he is looking for a job to do. Having your very own canine delivery service is an excellent way for your Patterdale Terrier to earn his keep. For this trick your pup has to pick up an object—a note, a tool, or any item reasonable for him to carry - and take it to someone else in the house.

1. Hand your Patterdale Terrier an object, using the command "Take It", and have the helper call him from a step or two away. Click and treat him for moving toward that person.

2. Gradually move the helper greater and greater distances and click and treat your Patterdale Terrier for moving away from you and toward your helper.

3. Gradually fade out the helper calling your Patterdale Terrier, having the person go out of sight.

4. Replace the "Take It" command with "Bring This to Daddy" (or whatever your helper's name is) by saying the new cue right before you say "Take It". Click and treat him for taking the object and moving in the direction of the helper. Gradually fade out the old cue.

5. Vary the objects you have your pup carry, and practice often - it will get better the more you practice it.

How did you get on? What challenges did you face & how did you overcome them? What could you do better for next time? **Any new discoveries?** Funny moments? *Memorable Photos?* **Sketches?**
Any other thoughts, comments or feedback

Mail a Letter

Teaching your Patterdale Terrier to mail a letter is a fun and functional trick that uses lots of energy and is very entertaining to watch. Your Patterdale Terrier must take a letter in his mouth, jump on the mailbox, and push the letter through the slot. He will need you to pull down the lever for him so he can drop the mail in the right spot.

1. Using the Touch command, ask your Patterdale Terrier to use his nose to push the letter into the slot. Click and treat him for touching his nose to the letter.

2. Withhold the click and treat until he pushes the letter a little further in the slot this time.

3. Have him put two front paws on the mailbox and click and treat him for staying up for gradually longer periods of time. If you have a Patterdale Terrier puppy, you may want to hold him close to the box and click him for putting his feet on the top.

4. Hand your Patterdale Terrier a letter and tell him to "Take It". Click and treat him for taking the letter, then for holding the letter for longer periods of time.

5. Call him to put his paws on the box while holding the letter, and click and treat.

6. Work on this step until he is easily balancing on his hind legs while holding the letter.

7. Now try to get him to leave the letter on the tray by telling him to "Leave It" and clicking and treating him for letting the letter go. You may need to adapt this trick for small dogs by holding them close to the box.

8. Practice all the steps until the entire trick is fluid and your Patterdale Terrier responds to your command "Take It" by following through with all the other steps.

9 Replace the cue "Take It" with the new cue "Mail It" by saying the new cue right before the old cue and gradually fading the old cue.

How did you get on? What challenges did you face & how did you overcome them? What could you do better for next time? **Any new discoveries?** Funny moments? *Memorable Photos?* **Sketches?**
Any other thoughts, comments or feedback

Throw This in the Trash

Teach your Patterdale Terrier to pick up anything you point at, including soda cans or other household items. This retrieving trick requires your Patterdale Terrier to pick up the trash and release the object into a trash bin. To make it easier for him to get the trash into the container, you will probably want to use an open or swing-top trash bucket that is no taller than your Patterdale Terrier's elbows.

Quick Tips: Don't Overturn the Trash Basket.

Consider the height of the trash basket and its opening when you are teaching this trick. The height of the basket needs to be proportionate to your Patterdale Terrier's head so the opening is easily accessible. As you add distance to this trick you may want to even add weight the basket so that it doesn't tip and scare your pup.

1. Work with your Patterdale Terrier and have him retrieve many different kinds of trash items; have him bring them to you over increasingly longer distances.

2. Sit on a chair with the trash bucket between your feet. Tell your Patterdale Terrier to pick up an item using the "Take It" cue, and call him to you; click and treat him when he is as close to the opening of the bucket as he will come.

3. Repeat this step but delay the click by a few seconds until he is eventually standing with his chin right over the edge of the bucket.

4. With your Patterdale Terrier standing close to the bucket, tell him to "Leave It" and click and treat him for releasing the trash. You will need to practice this so that your Patterdale Terrier will eventually release the item right into the trash bucket.

5. Experiment by withholding the click until your Patterdale Terrier makes a deliberate effort to drop the item in the bucket.

6. Label the behavior "Throw It Away" by saying this new cue right before the old cues "Take It" and "Leave It". You will have to practice this many times before the new cue initiates the behavior.

7. Practice with different items so that your Patterdale Terrier will retrieve and discard just about anything you ask him to.

Quick Tips: Take It to the Next Level

Just when you think you have covered all types of tricks - there are still more games and tricks to keep you and your pup learning new things together. These games are great to play in all sorts of places - in the backyard, at the beach, or in the living room. Your Patterdale Terrier is part of your family; if he's well trained and well behaved, he will get invited more places and will be more fun to be around.

How did you get on? What challenges did you face & how did you overcome them? What could you do better for next time? **Any new discoveries?** Funny moments? *Memorable Photos?* **Sketches?**
Any other thoughts, comments or feedback

Let's Play Ring Toss

This old-fashioned game is a wonderful way to occupy a high-energy Patterdale Terrier. You can buy an inexpensive ring-toss game in any toy or department store. For this trick your pup has to pick up each ring and place it on a post one at a time. This behavior is repeated until all three rings are on the post.

1. Hand your Patterdale Terrier a ring and click and treat him for holding it.

2. Place the pole close to you and have your Patterdale Terrier deliver the ring close to the post; click and treat him for releasing it over the post.

3. You may help him by tapping the post and encouraging him to drop it. Click and treat him for any attempts that he makes that result in the ring closer to the post.

4. Withhold the click and treat and only click attempts to put the ring on the post. With patience and time this can be a very entertaining game for your Patterdale Terrier to play.

How did you get on? What challenges did you face & how did you overcome them? What could you do better for next time? **Any new discoveries?** Funny moments? *Memorable Photos?* **Sketches?**
Any other thoughts, comments or feedback

Sea Hunt

For this trick your Patterdale Terrier has to fetch things out of a body of water. You can use a baby pool, the bathtub, a bucket, or a lake or pond. The goal for your pup is to retrieve all the items you sink or float and bring them back to dry land. This is a terrific warm-weather game because it gives your Patterdale Terrier a fun way to cool off. Fill up a baby pool with a few inches of water, depending on his size, and sink some treasures for him to retrieve. Here are the steps for teaching your Patterdale Terrier how to play Sea Hunt:

1. Hold the object on the surface and ask him to "Take It". Click and treat him for putting his mouth around it.

2. Hold the item just below the surface and click and treat him for dipping his nose under and taking it.

3. Gradually hold the item deeper until he is snagging it off the bottom.

4. Vary the types of things you have your Patterdale Terrier retrieve and keep the game light and fun.

5. Vary the depth of the water as he gets better at this game to make it more interesting and fun for everyone involved.

How did you get on? What challenges did you face & how did you overcome them? What could you do better for next time? **Any new discoveries?** Funny moments? *Memorable Photos?* **Sketches?**

Any other thoughts, comments or feedback

Achoo! Can I Have a Tissue?

This one is a real crowd pleaser. To perform this trick your Patterdale Terrier has to retrieve a tissue on a sneeze cue. And who wouldn't be impressed by a Patterdale Terrier that gets you a tissue when you sneeze? For this trick you need a popup box of tissues and a convincing fake sneeze.

1. Hand him a tissue and click and treat him for taking it and holding it.

2. Take a step away and have him bring it to you. Click and treat him for moving toward you with the tissue in his mouth.

3. Introduce the tissue box by pulling a tissue out and laying it across the top of the box. Click and treat him for taking the tissue off the top of the box.

4. Gradually tuck the tissue in so that he has to pull the tissue out to get his click and treat.

5. Replace the old cue "Take It" with the new cue "Achoo!" by saying the new cue right before the old cue. Click and treat your Patterdale Terrier for starting the behavior as you sneeze.

Quick Fix: What if your Patterdale Terrier is a shredder?

You can teach your Patterdale Terrier to grab a tissue without tearing it into a million pieces by giving him lots of opportunities to practice, and by not letting him hold the tissue for too long. It might also be a good idea to keep the tissue box in one place so he knows where to go to get a tissue when you sneeze.

Quick Tips: Get the Retrieving Show on the Road

Take retrieving on the road right away and you will both improve quickly because performing retrieving tricks in public is difficult. If you practice in different places from the start, your Patterdale Terrier will be comfortable retrieving anywhere.

How did you get on? What challenges did you face & how did you overcome them? What could you do better for next time? **Any new discoveries?** Funny moments? *Memorable Photos?* **Sketches?**
Any other thoughts, comments or feedback

Show Me Your Best Side

When your Patterdale Terrier is performing this trick, he looks as though he is posing for a picture. This trick requires him to turn his head to the side and hold it. The easiest way to teach this trick is by free shaping, which means limiting your Patterdale Terrier's options and catching the right behaviors with a click and treat to shape him into the actual position that you are looking for.

1. Start with your Patterdale Terrier facing you in a "Sit" and click and treat him for staying.

2. After about thirty seconds or so, stop clicking and watch him closely; if he turns his head at all, click and treat.

3. Pick one side or the other to start with and click any head turns in that direction.

4. When your Patterdale Terrier starts to understand that turning his head is causing the click, it's time to delay the click by a few seconds to encourage him to hold the position.

5. Gradually increase the seconds by a few at a time until he will turn his head to the side and hold it for fifteen seconds or so.

6. Label the behavior "Pose" just before he offers the turn of his head. Repeat until the command "Pose" causes the behavior.

How did you get on? What challenges did you face & how did you overcome them? What could you do better for next time? **Any new discoveries?** Funny moments? *Memorable Photos?* **Sketches?**

Any other thoughts, comments or feedback

Push a Baby Carriage

This trick is adorable, but for the sake of safety, it should not be practiced with a real baby - a doll carriage with a baby doll is safer. This trick requires your Patterdale Terrier to stand and walk on his hind legs while pushing the carriage with his front feet. The steps for teaching "Push a Baby Carriage" are as follows.

1. Get your Patterdale Terrier to sniff the baby carriage, and click and treat.

2. Secure the carriage so that it won't roll, and use a target to get your Patterdale Terrier to put his front paws on the handle; click and treat.

3. Get your Patterdale Terrier to hold the position by delaying the click and treat by a second or two.

4. Fix the carriage so that it will only roll a short distance (use blocks of wood behind the wheels), and click and treat your Patterdale Terrier for moving the carriage a little at a time.

5. Encourage him to move the carriage and click and treat him for complying.

6. Control how far the carriage rolls to avoid scaring your pup.

7. You can label this behavior "Push" by saying this cue as he is moving the carriage.

Quick Tip: Don't Tip the Carriage!

To prevent the carriage from tipping, weight the seat with some heavy books so that when your Patterdale Terrier jumps up to touch the handle, the carriage stays stable and stationary. Be sure the wheels are locked or use wood blocks to prevent the carriage from rolling away too soon.

How did you get on? What challenges did you face & how did you overcome them? What could you do better for next time? **Any new discoveries?** Funny moments? *Memorable Photos?* **Sketches?**
Any other thoughts, comments or feedback

Hi-Ho Silver, Away!

This trick is a great way to show off a Patterdale Terrier that likes to jump up on you. The only difference is your Patterdale Terrier is not making physical contact with you when he is holding the rearing-horse position with his front legs stretched upward. The steps for teaching "Hi-Ho Silver, Away!" are as follows:

1. Hold your hand as a target above your Patterdale Terrier's head and click and treat him for touching it.

2. Gradually raise your hand until he is all the way up on his hind legs.

3. Practice frequently to help him build up his leg muscles.

4. Get your Patterdale Terrier to hold the position by delaying the click and treat for several seconds.

5. Increase the time by a few seconds until he can hold the position for about fifteen seconds.

6. Cue your Patterdale Terrier to extend his paws by using the "Paw It" command with your hand as a target.

7. Only click and treat versions of this behavior that are of longer duration and the right position (front paws extended).

8. Fade the hand target by using it to start the behavior and then pulling it away. Click and treat your Patterdale Terrier for continuing to perform the behavior in the absence of the target.

9. Replace the old cue with the new cue "Away" by saying the new cue right before he starts the behavior.

How did you get on? What challenges did you face & how did you overcome them? What could you do better for next time? **Any new discoveries?** Funny moments? *Memorable Photos?* **Sketches?**
Any other thoughts, comments or feedback

Sit Up Pretty

For this trick your Patterdale Terrier sits on his hind legs with his front paws tucked into his chest. This is also a behavior that he needs to practice frequently to be able to build up his back and hind-end muscles. The steps for teaching "Sit Up Pretty" are as follows:

1. Use your hand as a target and click and treat him for touching your hand while raising his front end off the ground.

2. Withhold the click and treat by a few seconds to get your Patterdale Terrier to hold the position high enough to have him sitting up on his back end, but not standing.

3. Add a cue like "Sit Up" or "Beg", by saying it right before the "Touch" cue.

4. The click and treat should happen as soon as he starts the behavior on the new cue.

Quick Tips: Hand Fade

Practice fading your hand as a target by presenting it but clicking before he actually touches it. By clicking your Patterdale Terrier early so that he is on his way to touching your hand but doesn't actually make contact with it will mean that he will be less dependent on its presence and it will be easier to fade.

How did you get on? What challenges did you face & how did you overcome them? What could you do better for next time? **Any new discoveries?** Funny moments? *Memorable Photos?* **Sketches?**
Any other thoughts, comments or feedback

Balance a Cookie on Your Nose

This trick demonstrates your Patterdale Terrier's will power, because he must balance a cookie on his nose and wait to take the cookie until you say so.

1. Start with your Patterdale Terrier in a "Sit" in front of you and click and treat him for staying.

2. Practice holding his muzzle and placing a cookie on his nose for a click and treat.

3. Repeat this last step until he can hold still for several seconds.

4. Slowly let go of his muzzle and click and treat him for holding it steady.

5. Gradually increase the amount of time your Patterdale Terrier balances the cookie on his nose before you click and treat.

6. You will probably find after a bit of practice that he develops a flip-and-catch technique to eat the cookie. This makes the trick all the more flashy and impressive.

Quick Tips: Humble Patterdale Terriers

Although some Patterdale Terriers are prone to fancier tricks, others are, by nature, more sedate. These simple and adorable tricks suit more sedate personalities, and will therefore be easier for you to teach. How you use the tricks, such as "Say You're Sorry" is entirely up to you.

How did you get on? What challenges did you face & how did you overcome them? What could you do better for next time? **Any new discoveries?** Funny moments? *Memorable Photos?* **Sketches?**
Any other thoughts, comments or feedback

Say You're Sorry

For this trick your Patterdale Terrier lies down with his chin on the ground between his front paws. For an added bonus, teach him to look up at you, which will add an even more convincing element to the performance. You may want to use this as the canine version of "Time Out".

1. Put your Patterdale Terrier in a "Down" position, facing you; click and treat him for holding that position.

2. After around thirty seconds, withhold the click and wait. Pay close attention and click and treat any head motion down.

3. Once your Patterdale Terrier starts to understand that lowering his head is what causes the click, withhold the click until he holds the position for an extra second.

4. Increase the number of seconds your Patterdale Terrier has to keep his head down until you can build it up to fifteen to twenty seconds.

5. Label the behavior "Sorry" by saying the command right before he offers the behavior.

6. Repeat this step until the command "Sorry" triggers the behavior.

How did you get on? What challenges did you face & how did you overcome them? What could you do better for next time? **Any new discoveries?** Funny moments? *Memorable Photos?* **Sketches?**
Any other thoughts, comments or feedback

Say Your Prayers

Whether they are praying for leniency after getting into the garbage or praying for mud to roll in, any Patterdale Terrier looks cute performing this trick. This trick requires your Patterdale Terrier to rest his paws on a chair or stool and tuck his head between his front paws. He can be sitting or standing when he does this.

1. Use a table, stool, or chair that won't move when your Patterdale Terrier puts his paws on it.

2. Get your Patterdale Terrier to put his front paws on the stool by tapping the stool or luring him with a treat. Click any effort to get his paws up on the stool.

3. Delay the click so that your Patterdale Terrier is putting his paws up and leaving them there for three seconds before you click and treat.

4. Using a yogurt lid as a target, get your Patterdale Terrier to put his head between his front paws by placing the target slightly under his chest. Click and treat him for making attempts to touch the target.

5. Delay the click again until your Patterdale Terrier holds his nose to the target for longer periods of time.

6. Fade the target slowly by clicking before he actually touches it, or by making it smaller.

7. Label the behavior "Say Your Prayers" as he is performing the behavior, just before any other cues. Gradually fade any old cues.

Quick Tips: Prevent Sliding

To make the trick "Say Your Prayers" go more smoothly and to prevent your Patterdale Terrier from scaring himself, choose a low stool that he can put his paws up on easily - one that won't slide across the floor when he leans on it. Also consider doing this trick on a rug or potting non-skid material under the legs of the stool.

How did you get on? What challenges did you face & how did you overcome them? What could you do better for next time? **Any new discoveries?** Funny moments? *Memorable Photos?* **Sketches?**
Any other thoughts, comments or feedback

Ring a Bell

This trick involves teaching your Patterdale Terrier to ring a bell with his nose or a paw. This trick is also quite practical, as you can teach him to ring a bell when he wants to go outside to the bathroom.

Quick Tips: Patience Goes a Long Way

The critical factor to performing tricks successfully is your patience in handling your Patterdale Terrier. Using the skills you have learned so far, alongside your knowledge of chain methods, start training your Patterdale Terrier for these actions when you see that he is ready.

Hang a set of bells next to the door that you normally use to let your Patterdale Terrier outside. Once he learns how to ring the bell with his mouth or nose, start having him do this each time he goes out to go potty. Pretty soon your Patterdale Terrier will ring the bell to let you know he wants to go out.

You may want to use a set of sleigh bells for this trick; four or five bells on a long strap may make it easier for your Patterdale Terrier to learn to ring a bell, because it will give him more opportunities to be right.

The steps for teaching your Patterdale Terrier to "Ring a Bell" are as follows:

1. Put the bells on the floor and click and treat your Patterdale Terrier for sniffing them (you can use a "Touch" command if he knows one).

2. Delay the click and wait for him to touch harder or mouth them before you click and treat.

3. Work at this until he's ringing the bells with purpose.

4. Hang the bells next to the door and repeat the above steps until he is ringing them reliably.

5. Gradually increase the distance he must travel to touch the bells.

6. Verbally label ringing the bells, "Bells".

How did you get on? What challenges did you face & how did you overcome them? What could you do better for next time? **Any new discoveries?** Funny moments? *Memorable Photos?* **Sketches?**
Any other thoughts, comments or feedback

Dancing Patterdale Terrier

This trick is adorable but difficult for most Patterdale Terriers. To perform this trick, you Patterdale Terrier must balance on his hind legs and walk. You'll want to practice in short sessions to help him build up his back and leg muscles gradually. Be sure to work on a non-skid surface so that he does not injure himself. The steps for teaching "Dancing Patterdale Terrier" are as follows:

1. With your Patterdale Terrier in a Sit, hold your hand slightly above his nose and click and treat any effort to raise himself up on his back legs to touch your hand.

2. Raise your hand higher and continue to click and treat your Patterdale Terrier for using his hind end to raise himself up and touch your hand.

3. Get your Patterdale Terrier to hold the position longer by delaying the click by a second or two.

4. Gradually increase the time to several seconds.

5. Move your hand around and click and treat him for walking on his hind legs to touch it.

6. Turn your hand in a circle and click and treat your Patterdale Terrier for walking on his hind legs to follow it.

7. Add the cue "Dance" by saying it just before he starts the behavior.

How did you get on? What challenges did you face & how did you overcome them? What could you do better for next time? **Any new discoveries?** Funny moments? *Memorable Photos?* **Sketches?**
Any other thoughts, comments or feedback

Get Me a Bottle of Water - Part 1

This amazing trick involves your Patterdale Terrier opening the refrigerator, taking out a bottle of water, closing the door, and bringing the bottle of water to you. You'll probably want to start with a water bottle and then as he refines his techniques, you can change the water bottle to a can of soda or a bottle of juice. This trick has three different parts: retrieving the bottle, opening the refrigerator door, and closing the refrigerator door.

Getting the Water Bottle

1. Hand your Patterdale Terrier a bottle of water and tell him to "Take It". Click and treat him for hanging on to it for several seconds at a time.

2. Move away from your Patterdale Terrier and have him come to you over greater and greater distances. Click and treat him first as he is moving to you, and then for delivering the bottle to your hand.

3. Place the bottle on the floor and tell your Patterdale Terrier to "Take It", then "Bring It". Click and treat him for retrieving it, then gradually withhold the click until he is on his way back to you.

4. Put the bottle on a low shelf of the refrigerator and practice having him "Take It". Click and treat your Patterdale Terrier for at first approaching, then taking, then bringing the bottle to you over short training sessions.

Quick Fix: Use an Empty Can

Water bottles are the easiest to grasp at first, and later you can work up to retrieving cans or glass. If you have a Patterdale Terrier that tends to bite down hard when he retrieves things, you may want to practice with empty cans first to prevent him from scaring himself or making a mess of your kitchen.

How did you get on? What challenges did you face & how did you overcome them? What could you do better for next time? **Any new discoveries?** Funny moments? *Memorable Photos?* **Sketches?**
Any other thoughts, comments or feedback

Get Me a Bottle of Water - Part 2

Opening the Refrigerator Door

1. Put a strap on the refrigerator door to make it easier for your Patterdale Terrier to open it.

2. Starting with the refrigerator door open, hand your Patterdale Terrier the strap and tell him to "Take It". Click and treat him for taking the strap.

3. Once your Patterdale Terrier is taking the strap easily, delay the click for an extra second or two and click and treat him for holding it.

4. Standing slightly behind your Patterdale Terrier, call him back to you while he holds the strap. You may need to go back and teach him the formal retrieve with the strap or at least review it with him.

5. When he can hold on to the strap while backing up, click and treat him for actually moving the door.

6. Gradually close the door until it's almost clicked shut, so that he has to pull harder to open it.

7. Once your Patterdale Terrier can open it when it's shut all the way, try letting him retrieve the strap on his own. At first, click and treat any attempt to take the strap.

8. Gradually add a little distance so that he is approaching the refrigerator from greater and greater distances.

9. Eventually delay your click so that your Patterdale Terrier is taking the strap and starting to back up to pull the door open before you click. If at any time he seems confused and the behavior falls apart, go back and break things down into smaller parts and gradually rebuild the behavior.

How did you get on? What challenges did you face & how did you overcome them? What could you do better for next time? **Any new discoveries?** Funny moments? *Memorable Photos?* **Sketches?**
Any other thoughts, comments or feedback

Get Me a Bottle of Water - Part 3

Closing the Door Using His Nose

1. Once your Patterdale Terrier is comfortable holding the bottle in his mouth, practice having him target the refrigerator door with his nose.

2. Open the door a little, give a "Touch" command, and click and treat him for moving the door shut even a little.

3. Gradually leave the door open a little more until he is shutting the door with purpose. Make sure you click and treat your Patterdale Terrier even for small attempts to push the door shut.

4. Verbally label the behavior "Shut the Door".

Closing the Door Using His Paws

An alternate option would be to have your Patterdale Terrier use his paws on the refrigerator to close it.

1. Use a paw target to get him to touch the refrigerator with his paws, then click and treat.

2. Open the door a little and tell your Patterdale Terrier to paw the door; click and treat him for moving the door shut.

3. Gradually open the door more so your Patterdale Terrier has to push the door harder to earn the click and treat.

4. Verbally label the behavior "Shut the Door".

Review each piece before putting them all together. Open the refrigerator door (keep the bottle on the lower shelf), and have your Patterdale Terrier take the bottle. When he still has the bottle in his mouth, call him around the door and tell him to push it shut. Practice these two steps until they are fluid. Then add the command to "Take It" (the door strap), followed by retrieving the bottle. Practice these together until they are fluid. Then, combine them with closing the door. You may have to go back and forth a bit in order to keep each part of the behavior strong until eventually it is one continuous behavior.

How did you get on? What challenges did you face & how did you overcome them? What could you do better for next time? **Any new discoveries?** Funny moments? *Memorable Photos?* **Sketches?**
Any other thoughts, comments or feedback

Go Left, Go Right

Teaching your Patterdale Terrier how to distinguish from his left and right will amaze your friends and family. It will also enable you to direct your Patterdale Terrier to exactly where you want him to go.

1. Start with your Patterdale Terrier in front of an object (like a chair or a hassock) and put a target lid to the left of it about three feet away.

2. Send your Patterdale Terrier to go "Touch", and click and treat him for responding.

3. Repeat this at gradually increasing distances, clicking right before he touches his nose to the target.

4. When your Patterdale Terrier is offering the behavior readily, say the new cue "Go Left" just before he is about to move forward to touch the target. Repeat this until he will go to the left when you say "Left".

5. Fade the target by making it smaller (use scissors to cut it into smaller pieces) until your Patterdale Terrier simply moves left on command.

6. To teach your Patterdale Terrier to go right, simply follow all the same steps except with everything on the right.

You can combine the "Go Left" and "Go Right" commands with retrieving tricks by lining up several objects in a row and asking your Patterdale Terrier to take the one on the left or the right. If nothing else, this trick will give you a better foundation for teaching him more complicated tricks.

How did you get on? What challenges did you face & how did you overcome them? What could you do better for next time? **Any new discoveries?** Funny moments? *Memorable Photos?* **Sketches?**

Any other thoughts, comments or feedback

Find It

Sending your Patterdale Terrier to find something you have lost is useful and exciting to both parties. Losing your wallet or keys in a pile of leaves or along your walking route could be disastrous - unless your Patterdale Terrier can help with the search.

1. Choose an item with lots of your scent on it (like a hat or a hair tie) and show it to your Patterdale Terrier.

2. Have someone hold your Patterdale Terrier's collar while you hide the item somewhere obvious at first.

3. Release him to go find it and click and treat him as he approaches it.

4. Gradually increase the difficulty by hiding it in more challenging places.

5. Find another item to practice with and try again.

6. Label the behavior "Find It" as your Patterdale Terrier moves toward the object.

How did you get on? What challenges did you face & how did you overcome them? What could you do better for next time? **Any new discoveries?** Funny moments? *Memorable Photos?* **Sketches?**
Any other thoughts, comments or feedback

Weave Poles

Weaving through poles is part of agility competition courses. It is a really nice way to teach control and focus at home.

You don't need to buy expensive agility equipment to teach this, some garden canes will do.

1. Begin by sticking your canes into the ground, in a straight line, with a gap between each of them of about twice your Patterdale Terrier's body width.

2. The easiest way to teach your Patterdale Terrier to weave between the poles is to guide him with your target stick or a reward. You can have him walking at your heel between you and the weave poles so that your body beside him will encourage a straight line.

3. Remember to add the word "weave" as he is learning and reinforce every stage of his progress with plenty of reward.

How did you get on? What challenges did you face & how did you overcome them? What could you do better for next time? **Any new discoveries?** Funny moments? *Memorable Photos?* **Sketches?**
Any other thoughts, comments or feedback

Jump Hurdle

Teaching your Patterdale Terrier to jump over a hurdle is another part of agility training. It can be any hurdle and you will not need to buy any special equipment to do this either. I taught our family Patterdale Terrier to hurdle, as a child, simply with rocks and a cane.

1. Start your training with a low hurdle, one that your pup can step over, and ask him to stay facing the jump whilst you walk around it, or go over it, and turn to face him.

2. Show your Patterdale Terrier a treat and call him over the jump and as he leaves the ground, reinforce and give him the treat as he reaches you.

3. You can just as easily use your target stick to guide him over the jump. By doing it this way you can walk alongside him as he jumps.

4. Now you have given him the idea you can introduce your command word and practice with different jumps and heights. Ensure that your Patterdale Terrier can manage the height of the existing jump before making it higher.

How did you get on? What challenges did you face & how did you overcome them? What could you do better for next time? **Any new discoveries?** Funny moments? *Memorable Photos?* **Sketches?**
Any other thoughts, comments or feedback

Through Hoop/Tunnel

Teaching your Patterdale Terrier to go through something such as a hoop or tunnel will improve his confidence greatly. The hoop can be anything, a tire or even a home-made tunnel. Pet stores often sell pet tunnels at a reasonable price.

1. Ask your Patterdale Terrier to sit and wait and place a treat on the ground in front of him, at a distance of about one meter.

2. Now put the tunnel or hoop between him and his treat, and perimeter on the ground so that he simply walks through it to fetch his treat. Then tell him it's OK to get his reward.

3. You could also use the target stick for this and simply guide your Patterdale Terrier through the obstacle with its tip.

4. Reinforce as he steps through the hoop and offer a second reward after he has collected the first.

5. You can now begin to add the command word and soon you will be able to send your Patterdale Terrier through the obstacle.

How did you get on? What challenges did you face & how did you overcome them? What could you do better for next time? **Any new discoveries?** Funny moments? *Memorable Photos?* **Sketches?**
Any other thoughts, comments or feedback

Weave Through Legs

I once came third in a dog show after teaching my middle aged Labrador to do this trick. It looks fantastic, most impressive and is reasonably easy to teach. You never know it could also earn your pup a rosette.

1. Have your Patterdale Terrier on your left hand side, show him a treat in your right hand then lift your right leg for him to go through and fetch the treat. This can also be done with a target stick but is easier initially to use the treats.

2. When your Patterdale Terrier weaves through your first leg reinforce the action with your normal reinforcement sound.

3. You can now make the movement of another step and lure him back through that leg, reinforcing and rewarding as needed.

4. Gradually increase your pace in order to teach him that he can weave through your legs when you walk normally. Then add your command word, such as weave or knit, and keep practicing.

How did you get on? What challenges did you face & how did you overcome them? What could you do better for next time? **Any new discoveries?** Funny moments? *Memorable Photos?* **Sketches?**
Any other thoughts, comments or feedback

Jump Through Arms

This one looks really impressive and any Patterdale Terrier that can leap through his owners arms will look like a professional trickster. In fact this is so easy to teach in a few confidence building steps that you may be surprised;

1. As with any other jumping trick, the idea is to begin the practice of the jump low down where it is not too intimidating for him.

2. See if you can enlist the help of a friend or family member for this initial stage then kneel down side on to your Patterdale Terrier and place your arms in a loop low to the ground then ask your helper to lure your Patterdale Terrier through your arms with a treat, when your pup is halfway through, reinforce and allow your helper to reward him

3. It's as simple as that. Then when your Patterdale Terrier is confident and knows what to do, you can raise your arms in order to make the jump more complicated. Add the command word and gently progress until you can kneel and then stand whilst your Patterdale Terrier jumps through the loop in your arms.

How did you get on? What challenges did you face & how did you overcome them? What could you do better for next time? **Any new discoveries?** Funny moments? *Memorable Photos?* **Sketches?**

Any other thoughts, comments or feedback

www.ingramcontent.com/pod-product-compliance
Lightning Source LLC
Chambersburg PA
CBHW030448010526
44118CB00011B/851